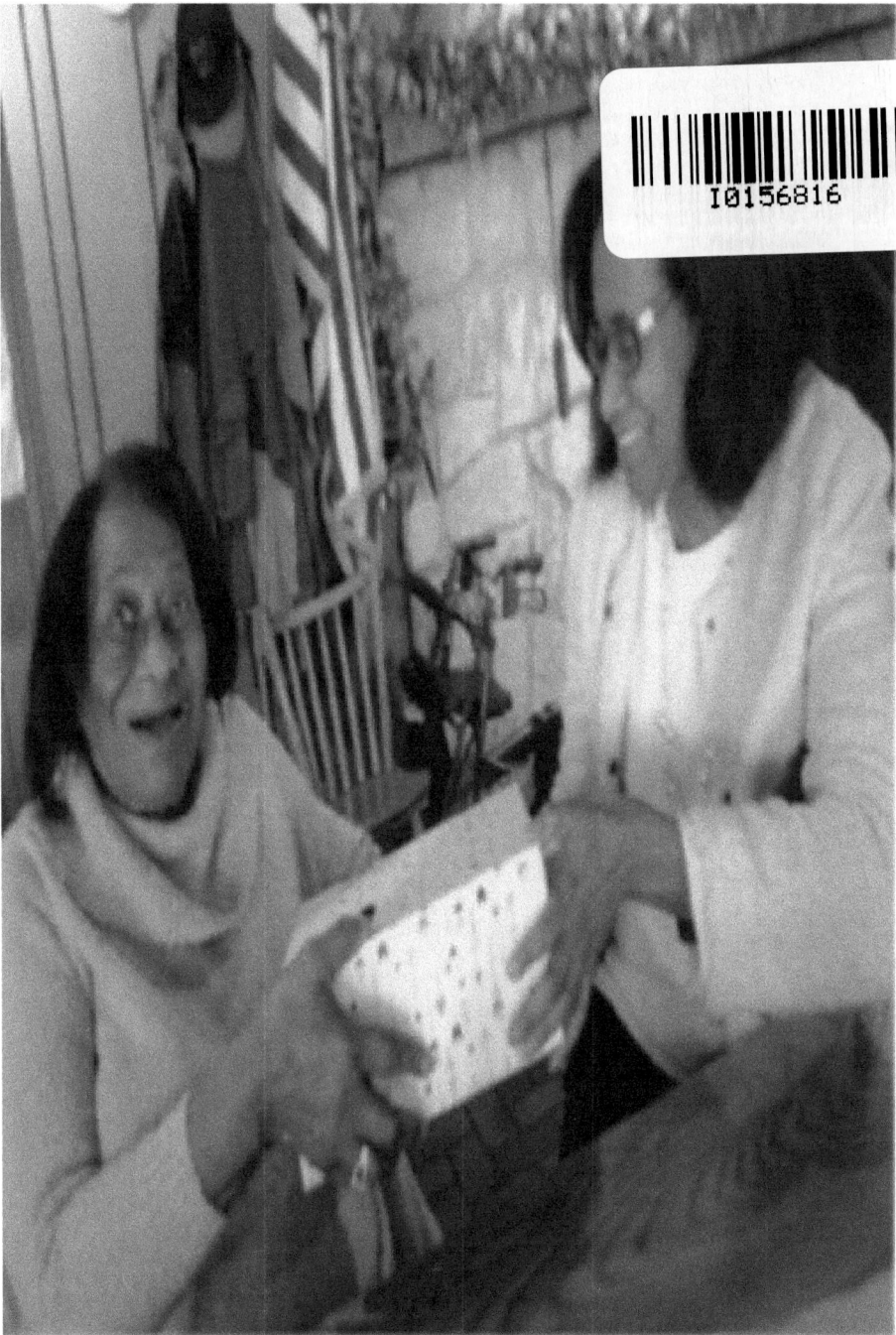

[In this moment, Mama passed the legacy of poetry - the treasured box - to me.]

*The Treasured Box*

# The Treasured Box

## A Loving Literary Collection Of Estelle Beasley Turner

## Compiled By Kathleen Estelle Joiner

# Dedication
To the Legacy of Great Grandmother
Estelle Beasley Turner

On behalf of my Great-grandmother Estelle, this book is dedicated to all the treasured box holders.

No matter your age, title or position, recognize that you hold gifts the world is just waiting for you to share. Discover those gifts in your heart and DNA ... in your own treasured box.

The Bible says parents should leave a heritage for their children. Whether or not the legacy is monetary, it should always include solid faith in God, hard work, gratitude, compassion, intentional consistency, and resilience. Those intangible yet priceless traits serve as benchmarks when your journey gets tumultuous. The seeds you plant establish the legend that remains.

I dedicate this to Mama, the tender caregiver of her grandmother's "treasure box" then passing it to me 15 years ago. In that simple moment, Mama entrusted me to be the guardian of this priceless, treasured gift to enjoy and publish. Now the legacy lives on.

So thankful for God's caring Hand and angels of protection so she can now hold the gems from her grandmother's poetry box. Mama, I hope it brings you joy.

And finally, to my family, children and friends, thanks for filling me with your love, prayers, and support. So fulfilling to see you smitten with the writing "love bug." Keep writing.

It's your story. Truly, no one can tell it like you.

# Foreword and Biography

This book is a compilation of poetry written by Estelle Beasley Turner, the paternal grandmother of my mother, Gloria Beasley Dabney. Mom gave them to me in a box, some 15 years ago after receiving them from her step-mother, Mildred Beasley. She knew we both loved writing. But little did I know the box was brimming with original handwritten poetry. What a treasured box!

Great grandmother Estelle was born September 26, 1889, in Shreveport, Louisiana. She loved literary greats such as Ralph Waldo Emerson, Henry David Thoreau.

She enjoyed the quietness of the morning, while being serenaded by the birds' morning praise. The dew soaked her spirit with words of encouragement, before the world awoke and became hurried.

She was an excellent cook and baker. Mama still raves about her mouth-watering coconut cakes. She hosted many tea parties, enjoyed concerts, symphonies. Simple living, friendships, truth, and honesty were a priority.

An award-winning poetess, Estelle Beasley Turner was a weekly columnist for the Oakland Tribune. Her church, Beth Eden Baptist Church, was treated to her unending literary gifts that she shared on many occasions. Although I have many original poems, her poetry collection is housed in the African American Museum of the Oakland, CA library.

Simply, she shared her gift of encouragement with as many as possible before she died May 14, 1961 in Oakland, CA. Although I was a youngster when she died, I am astonished at how our writing style is so similar. Our passion for writing is identical. Listening to the Lord's voice is in our DNA.

Once boxed away in storage, great grandmother's penned words are now printed for sharing. The baton has been passed and the legend lives on. The world is richer because of it.

*The Treasured Box*

# The Treasured Box
## Table of Contents

*(A copy of handwritten draft of "A Box Seat
at the Opera.")*

# My Visitor Loves Sugar Cookies

Below me lives a little boy
About two or three if not more
He clambers up my high back stairs
Stands tapping at my door.

I know, and love to hear that tap
My door I open wide
Without a word he stands and
smiles
Then quickly steps inside.

Bright eyes like search lights sweep around
They need not travel far
There upon the table in plain view
Sits my sugar cookie jar.

With a cookie in each chubby hand
He starts towards the door, but I bar the way
I reach and clasp him tightly in my arms
And say I'd like to have my pay.

He worms and squirms to be released
It's my pay and I never miss
He knows the price, so then he plants
On my cheek, a sweet, wet kiss.

# To Our Visitors

Our door of welcome is open wide
To all who would enter in.
To welcome you with joy and pride
The Savior waits within.

May we ever offer what pleases Him
Holy hymns of joyous praise,
Humble prayers of faith to God,
The keeper of all our ways.

Join in the worship fully free
To speak, to sing, to pray,
As the Spirit bids, now be moved
On this our dear Lord's day.

## Our Church

A tiny twig, in fertile soil into a healthy supine grew
Its beauty and its promise, the woodman instinctively
knew.
Though buffed and beaten through the winter night
By fierce and wildest storm
Still raised its head in triumph
To greet the early morn.

Today she stands majestically a tree,
To take her place,
To clear her spreading branches;
She is seeking more space.

## The Lone Gander

In circles searching the autumn sky
Wearily winging his way
Wonder on wonder, flying high

In the near dawned, crispy, clear day.

Lost from the flock, southward found
They are gone; they have left no trace
No marked trail, no course to be found.
Lost in the sea of space.

# The Bird And I

As I sit out here, on my small back porch
And smile in the warm sunshine,
When a small bird sings from his clothesline perch
Such rhythm is calling rhyme.

In weather tented coat his head held high,
He sings a note from the King
There in the bluing sky
Is the sun-bright face of Spring.

Unmindful of me, as I am of he,
Pegasus comes sailing by;
One spring I'm astride, and off for a ride
With words and music together, we sing, the bird and I.

# I Would Sing Of Love

If I had a private store of words at my command,
Words of which I could be sure all folks could
understand
I'd set these words to music sweet, I'd sing aloud –
I'd sing – the chorus over and over,
Repeating as birds sing of the Spring.

If I had a station all my own, I'd broadcast day and
night,
I'd sing of love and love alone.

I'd sing with all my might.

I would be heard the whole world 'round.
Then pause and listen to hear,
Some back to me, the echoing sound,
Love – real loud and clear.

# In Those Days

Men walked in groups, in clusters they stood.
In awe and in sadness wherever they would
All mirthful profits were taken from the air.
Still there was hope and there was comfort
In hymn and in prayer.

A dazzling brightness, shown in the light of the Sun,
As of glorifying a work well done.

Men are praying now as before ever prayed,
In the life that had passed, all their hopes were stayed.

Now it is up to God in his distress he will turn,
Earnestly seeking His will now to learn.

Great men with the ages have passed on their way
Yet God is still with us as we walk day by day.

# Know The Truth

May all our cares be blown away like fallen leaves on
an autumn day
May our hopes be as stayed as the sequoias are old

May our faith shine as bright as the Ophiro's gold
May our love be as true, as the sun will shine
After the clouds are broken away
Perfect as the Father, who loves us, no matter how far
we stray.

May we keep our steps attune with our God-given
being
Where that dread enemy, fear, has no place;
Where hope and trust blend in accord

Where love and joy never go abroad,
Where the truth that sets us free, we embrace.

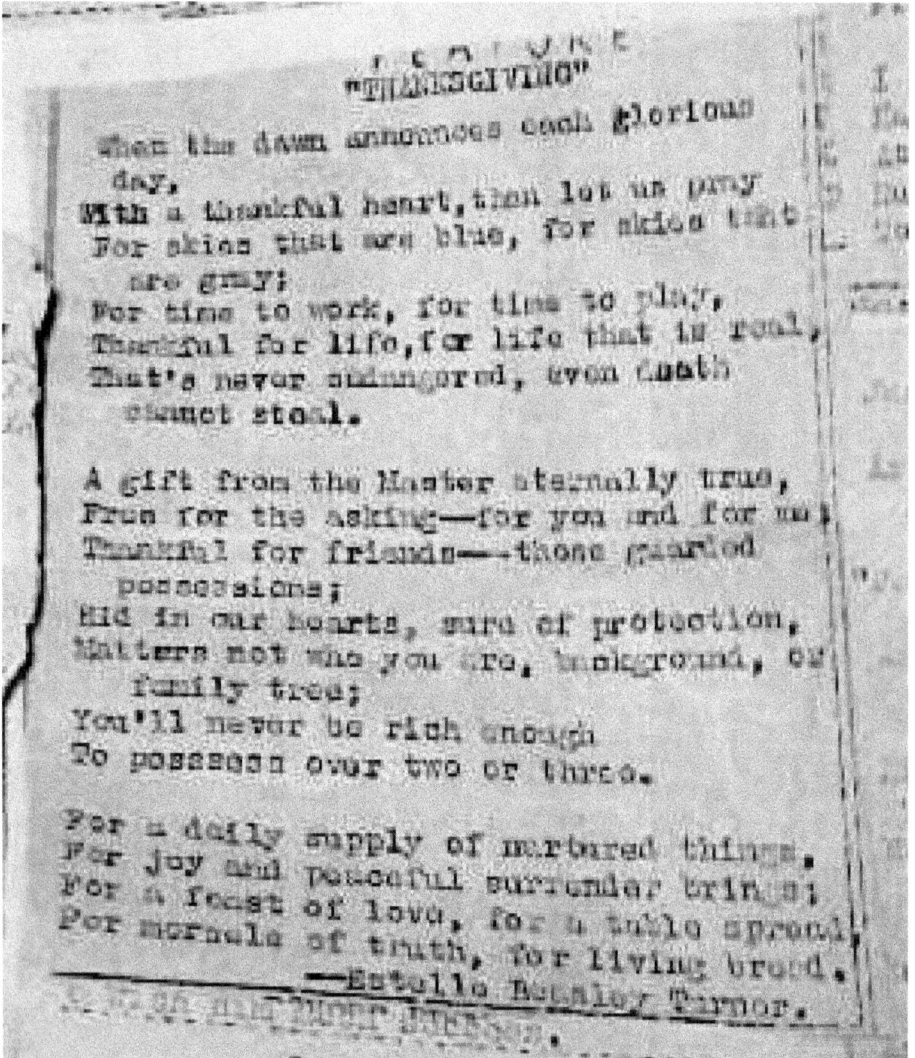

(Newspaper copy of "Thanksgiving" poem)

# Thanksgiving

When the dawn announces each glorious day,
With a thankful heart, then let us pray
For skies that are blue, for skies that are gray
For time to work, for time to play.
Thankful for life, for life that is real,
That's never endangered, even death cannot steal.

A gift from the Master, eternally true,
Free for the asking – for me and for you.
Thankful for friends – those guarded possessions;
Hid in our hearts, sure of protection,

Matters not who you are, background, or family tree;
You'll never be rich enough
To possess over two or three.

For a daily supply of nurtured things,
For joy and peaceful surrender brings;
For a feast of love, for a table spread,
For morsels of truth, for living bread.

# The Peace The Angels Sang About

The peace the angels sing about,
Comes from within not without.
Not as a garment one can put on,
But from the hearts of lives new born.

The brightness of the star is seen
Only by those who follow the gleam
Of truth that leads to love divine.

Earnestly seeking the Christ we will find
Then we will share our gifts with others
Joy and peace,
With all men, our brothers.

## Gifts

Around this time each passing year,
We turn our thoughts to gifts of cheer
To those who are with us and those far away.
To be opened with joy and laughter on Christmas Day.

Let there be found in each package tied
A generous portion of love inside,
May the light that shines from each tinseled tree
Send a radiance of love over land and sea.

Love, the greatest gift of all,
That first Christmas morn we now recall.
God the all good, from heaven above,
Sent us a gift from heaven, the son of his love.

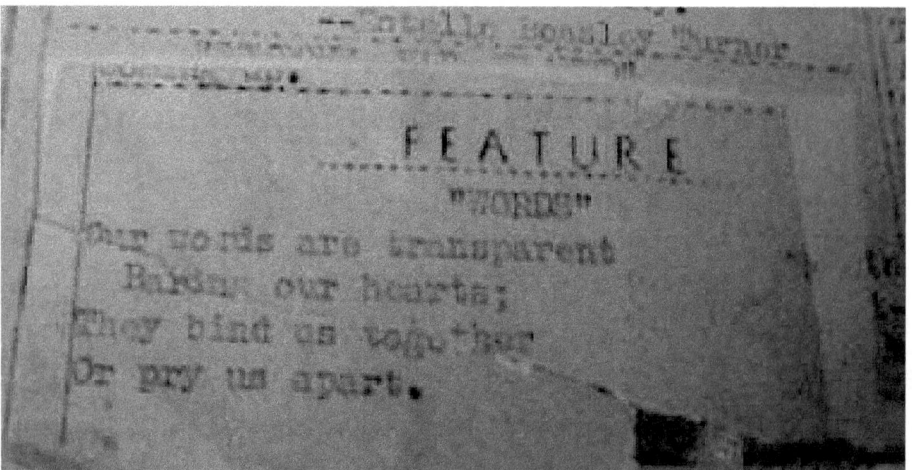

*(Newspaper copy of "Words" poem)*

*Estelle Beasley Turner*

## Did You Forget Someone?

Someone long since forgotten
Someone so near and oh so dear
Someone who always loves you
Every day throughout the year.

With never a kindly remembrance
In return for all you have received
Yet He waits and forgives your negligence
Although His kind heart be very grieved.

To friends far and near, you find greetings Your gifts of
silver and gold
Forgetting the Christ that brought us Christmas
And eternal life to the soul.

## The Evening Stroll

In the evening hour, the mind can stroll
Through the hedge of day and be made whole.
For a welcome presence – no eye can see –
Is singing, singing constantly.

Losing the day's outmoded coat,
Now we rise and float above...
The narrow border time
Into a higher climb.

Confident, night leisures along,
Closing the gate, my friend is gone.
But we will meet again –until then –
I have minted words to feed my pen.

# Your Hand

It gives me joy and confidence, the strong grasp of
your hand
I find therein the evidence. I feel, you understand.

When sunshine fills my pleasant way, in your hand I
find joy complete,
When the wild storm heats, so dark the day,
Your warm handshake says, 'no defeat.'

Then comes to each, to one and all, the time that will
ask for the test
The day when no work you can recall, your handshake,
will say it best.

It gives my joy and confidence, the strong grasp of
your hand,
It brings to me the evidence, you always understand.

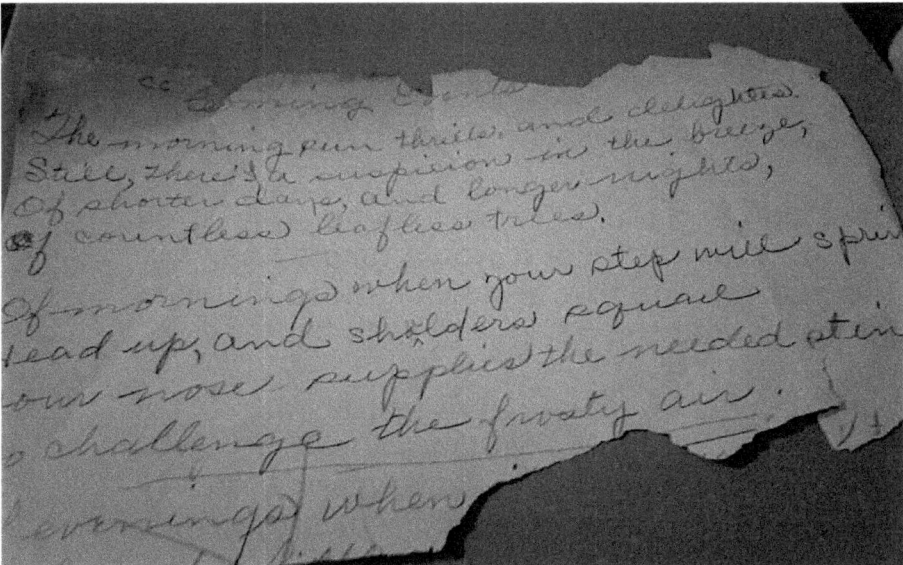

*(Handwritten copy of "Coming Events" poem)*

## Glory Only In The Cross

God forbid that we should glory –
If all the world was ours to share;
All the good we had hoped of doing
We could do with much to spare.

Should our faith as Jacob's ladder,
Span the space from earth to sky, faith to move
mountains of error
With just a flicker of an eye.

Our lights held high, burning brightly,
As silver flares against the night
Courage to fell acute temptation, never swerving from
the right..

God forbid that we should glory
Only in our Savior's cross
There the whole account was settled.
All our good becomes but dross.

## A Traveler Reaches Home

The rising Sun found her well on her way
The journey was long, it would take all day.
The path was narrow, she would need a guide
So she sought the Saviour to walk by her side.

When curves of danger were just ahead
"Lord, take my hand," to Him she said;
When strength was spent, and weary worn,
She leaned on His arm, supported, safe from harm.

The Noon day's Sun beamed in its full strength,
She walked in His shadow, cool and content;

When disappointments, sorrows; fled from His smile,
Came this kindly reminder, "I'm with you, my child."

Then came the evening, twilight descends,
The end of the trail, the journey's end
The gates swing open, then softly close,
Then comes repose, sweet repose.

## Sincere Desire

Let me forget dear Lord, today the things that would
annoy,
Those little things that creep around; to steal me from
my joy.

Be there no false notes in my song, let harmony fill my
heart.
Through love and praise and these alone, we see Thee
is thou art.

Then will I in thee rejoice, forgetting self and pride
Know the peace surrender brings, in Thee will I abide.

So let me work each day for Thee, each Sabbath to
return,
There to thy house to be refilled
Of Thee, Lord, more to learn.

## Watch Your Step

Perfect feet are much admired
When in fitted shoes attired.

They may bring fame and fortune too
But be careful where they carry you!

# The Reading

There were no prize words in the poem
Not a verb to rate or merit,
What brought that long and loud applause
Is the tasty way she read it!

# Tell-Tale Words

When we say, "I'll do my best,"
We had better be very careful as what we do in that case
May be a tasty mouthful.

And when we say, "There's a little good," in all the human family;
Remember we are all on the spot
Those words might come in handy.

And when we say, "It's the gospel truth," it is we hope to die!
The truth will stand without a crutch,
We need not signify.

And when we say, "I told you so I knew it would leak out,"
Be sure we did not have a part
In spreading it around and about.

So, it is true, these tell-tale words can play the tragic part
And through their clear transparency
We often glimpse the heart.

## Had You Walked With Me

Had you walked with me so early
As morning came in her quiet way
When flowers lift their fresh washed faces
Each little bird had his own say.

Beauty came also with her,
Coyly blushing by her side,
The sleepy hills drew their curtains
To watch the two go strolling by.

Had shared with me that holy something
A wish, to rise, to lift, to sing,
Alive, awake, each golden moment
To carry the colors of the King.

Had you walked with me so early,
The glory that I failed to see
Would have been yours, and you the richer
If only you had walked with me.


## Friendship

When old friends assemble to welcome the new
Into that golden circle that have seen
the years through
Years that have sifted all alloy away
Leaving the fine gold, there, forever to stay.

Old friends are unworried, when the truth misconstrued
About something you have spoken,
the new might be confused
The old knows you are not perfect
and still they know too
These are some things that you would never say or do.

What old friends so well know, the new friends must learn
The secret of true friendship is friends must be true in return.

## The Value Of A Friend

Who can weigh the value of a friend
Time-balanced and known to be true
Through challenging circumstances

Flame tested and proven pure
A bond that will not bend or break
Each link of Ophirs finest gold
Form this strong and shining chain
That will not fail, will ever hold.

Our friends are chosen gifts from God
A close knitting of souls here told
These beauty blended fadeless cords
Are fresh and new; are rich and old.

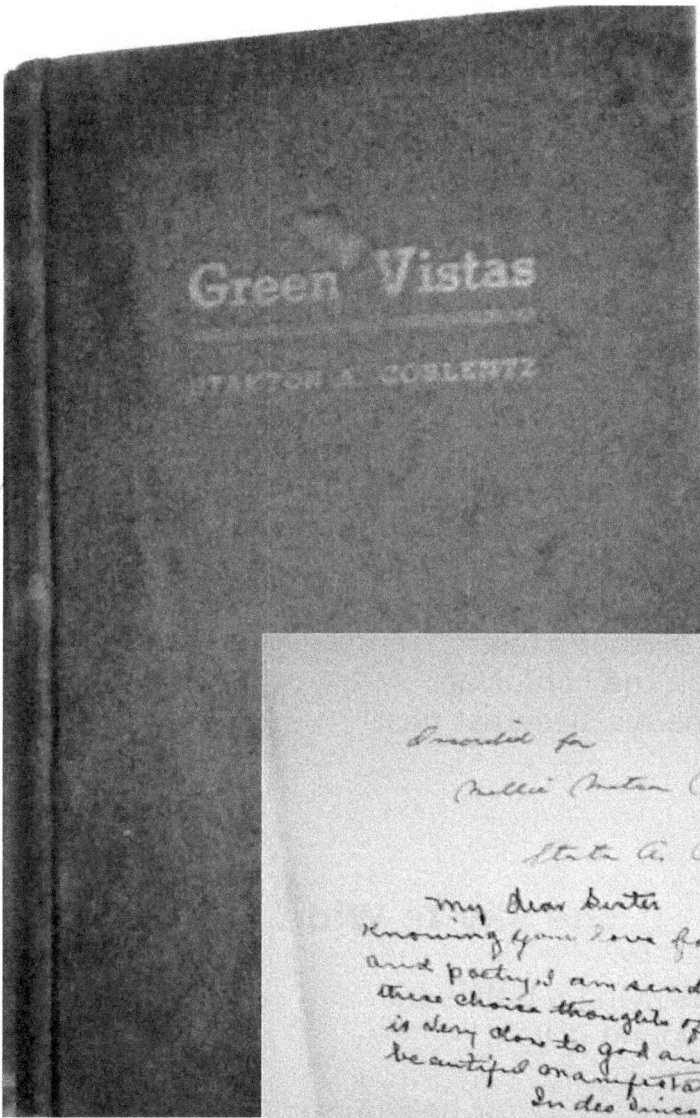

*(The book, Green Vistas, is signed by its author, Stanton Coblentz; inscribed for Mildred Beasley who eventually gave it to Great Grand-mother Estelle.)*

# Childhood Method

He wanted to help his Mommy
It would make her feel real proud.
He thought he'd do the living room
And no one was even allowed ...
To offer any suggestion, just how he was to start.
Behind closed doors he proceeded to take the room
apart.

Dusted books were scattered around,
brushed cushions here and there,
Even now she is wondering how he moved every chair.

He called, "Come look, see Mommy!"
This was the mother's test
To see through the confusion
That he'd done his sweetest best!

# The Sky Is Wide

There he goes flying a Sabre jet
Swifter than sound is light

We shudder, then smile for he's our own,
Yet still we think how he might

Be a strong, ambitious alien boy
Equipped and devil sent
Trusted by those of an evil cause
With hell's finest instrument!

# My Ambition

Let me do my little job so well,
That I'm given a bigger one,
Let me grow so nicely in the shade
That I'm given a chance in the Sun.

Let me fill my little place so full,
With love and gratitude,
Till forced into a bigger one
Won by humble servitude.

When I've known what mortals call success,
Let me be not proud, but meek,
Let me never puff, or vaunt myself,
My work for me will speak.

# Resolved

To build again upon the ruins
Of last year's resolutions,
And use my failure
As the stone
Found in the desolation.

Forget the sting that caused the pain
When honest pledge was broken.
Forget the taste of bitter words
Hastily spoken.

To stand as porter at the door
Keep vagrant thoughts away
That only ramble round and spoil,
Making more work for the day.

RESOLVED – to find that open door
Where want and woe holds sway;
No well walked path to mark the spot,
Enter there and serve that day.

When morning brings her priceless gift
God's first creation – LIGHT!
Fulfill her hours, unless I've tried
To know, and do, the right.


## The Gift

'Twas just a bit of crockery
Made into a tiny vase,
Given me by a little girl,
With a sweet smile on her face.

'Twas the way that she presented it,
The look within her eyes,
The vase seemed to shine as gold,
Appearing three times its real size.

A flower sometimes you'll be finding,
Said she that will just fit this vase,
Surely you'll find a place for it.
It really won't take up much space.

"Thank you" said I, with gladness,
Born only by spiritual power,
"As a little child" she  possessed it,
Susan, herself was the flower.

## Coming Events

The morning sun thrills and delights
Still, there's a suspicion in the breeze,
Of shorter days and longer nights,
Of countless leafless trees.

Of mornings when your step will spring,
Heads up and shoulders square
Your nose supplies the needed sting
To challenge the frosty air.

## Related

My strong appreciation of you
Tells me that I have something too
That catches the spark flying from your flame
Alike and still, far from the same.

A relative from your father's side
A keen kinship that holds, well tied
Not counted as close, I know that's true
I am yet proud that I am related to you.

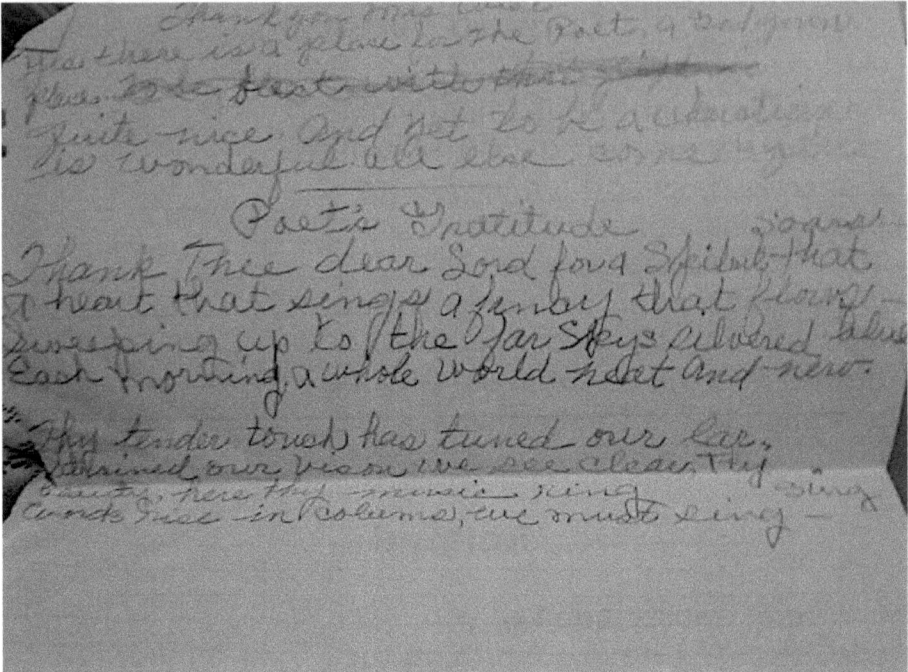

(Handwritten copy of "Poet's Gratitude" poem)

## Poet's Gratitude

Thank Thee, dear Lord for a spirit that soars
A heart that sings, a fancy that floors
Sweeping up to the far skies, silver and blue
Each morning a whole world, neat and new.

Thy tender touch has tuned our ear
Strained our focus, we now see clear
Thy beauty; hear thy music ring
Words rise in columns, we must now sing!

Yes, there is a place for the poet, a God-given space.
A habitation; filled with mercy and grace
to finish this race.

# Afterword

And so the legacy continues ...

The box of poetry symbolizes the "box" of treasured passions and purpose that resides in us.  These ancestral gifts have been embedded in our DNA, coded to fulfill our destiny.

Dad was a Navy and Air Force veteran, an engineer, community leader and an advocate for youth and senior citizens.  His predominant passion was education. Mom loves flowers, plants, excels in creative thinking, planning, organizing, and cooking. She and Dad shared the love of faith, family, and a spirit of excellence, education, art, and baking.

From the eldest of the eight siblings to the youngest; and their children, the shared gifts are evident.

The box, brimming with gems, have become generational treasures to continue the legacy.

*Kathleen Joiner*

# Legacy of Estelle Beasley-Turner

**Great Grandmother
Estelle Beasley Turner**

**William
Beasley**

**Grace Dell
Owens-Neely**

**Gloria
Beasley-Dabney**

**Clarence
Wellborn Dabney**

**Philip
Dabney**

**Michael
Dabney**

**Roanna
LaCour**

**Margaret
Dabney**

**Kathleen
Joiner**

**Paul
Dabney**

**Christopher
Dabney**

**Steven
Dabney**

# Ancestors of Gloria Beasley-Dabney

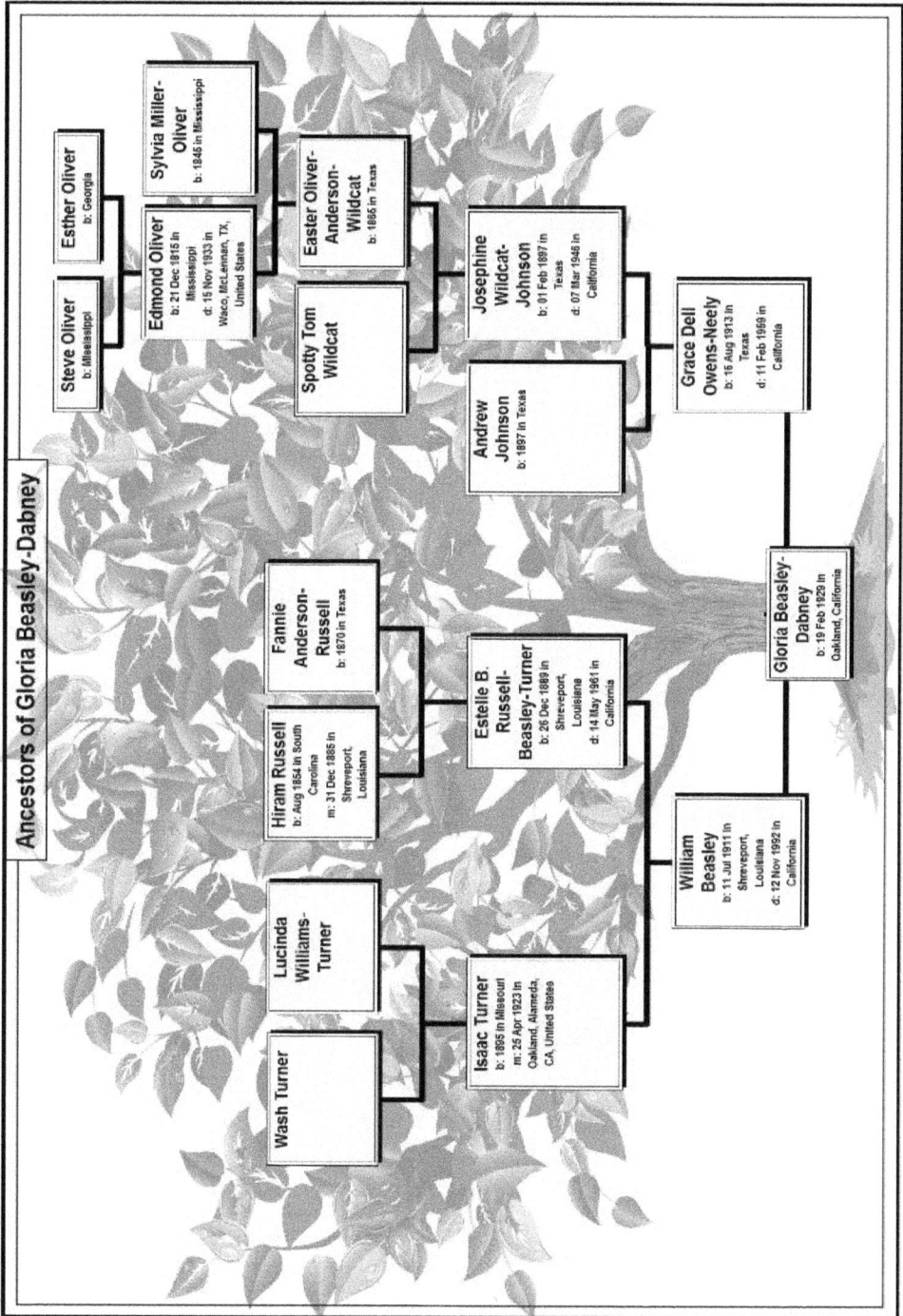

**Ancestors of Gloria Beasley-Dabney**

**Esther Oliver**
b: Georgia

**Sylvia Miller-Oliver**
b: 1845 in Mississippi

**Steve Oliver**
b: Mississippi

**Edmond Oliver**
b: 21 Dec 1815 in Mississippi
d: 15 Nov 1933 in Waco, McLennan, TX, United States

**Easter Oliver-Anderson-Wildcat**
b: 1865 in Texas

**Spotty Tom Wildcat**

**Josephine Wildcat-Johnson**
b: 01 Feb 1897 in Texas
d: 07 Mar 1946 in California

**Andrew Johnson**
b: 1897 in Texas

**Grace Dell Owens-Neely**
b: 16 Aug 1913 in Texas
d: 11 Feb 1969 in California

**Fannie Anderson-Russell**
b: 1870 in Texas

**Hiram Russell**
b: Aug 1854 in South Carolina
m: 31 Dec 1885 in Shreveport, Louisiana

**Estelle B. Russell-Beasley-Turner**
b: 26 Dec 1889 in Shreveport, Louisiana
d: 14 May 1961 in California

**Lucinda Williams-Turner**

**Wash Turner**

**Isaac Turner**
b: 1895 in Missouri
m: 25 Apr 1923 in Oakland, Alameda, CA, United States

**William Beasley**
b: 11 Jul 1911 in Shreveport, Louisiana
d: 12 Nov 1992 in California

**Gloria Beasley-Dabney**
b: 19 Feb 1929 in Oakland, California

*The Treasured Box*

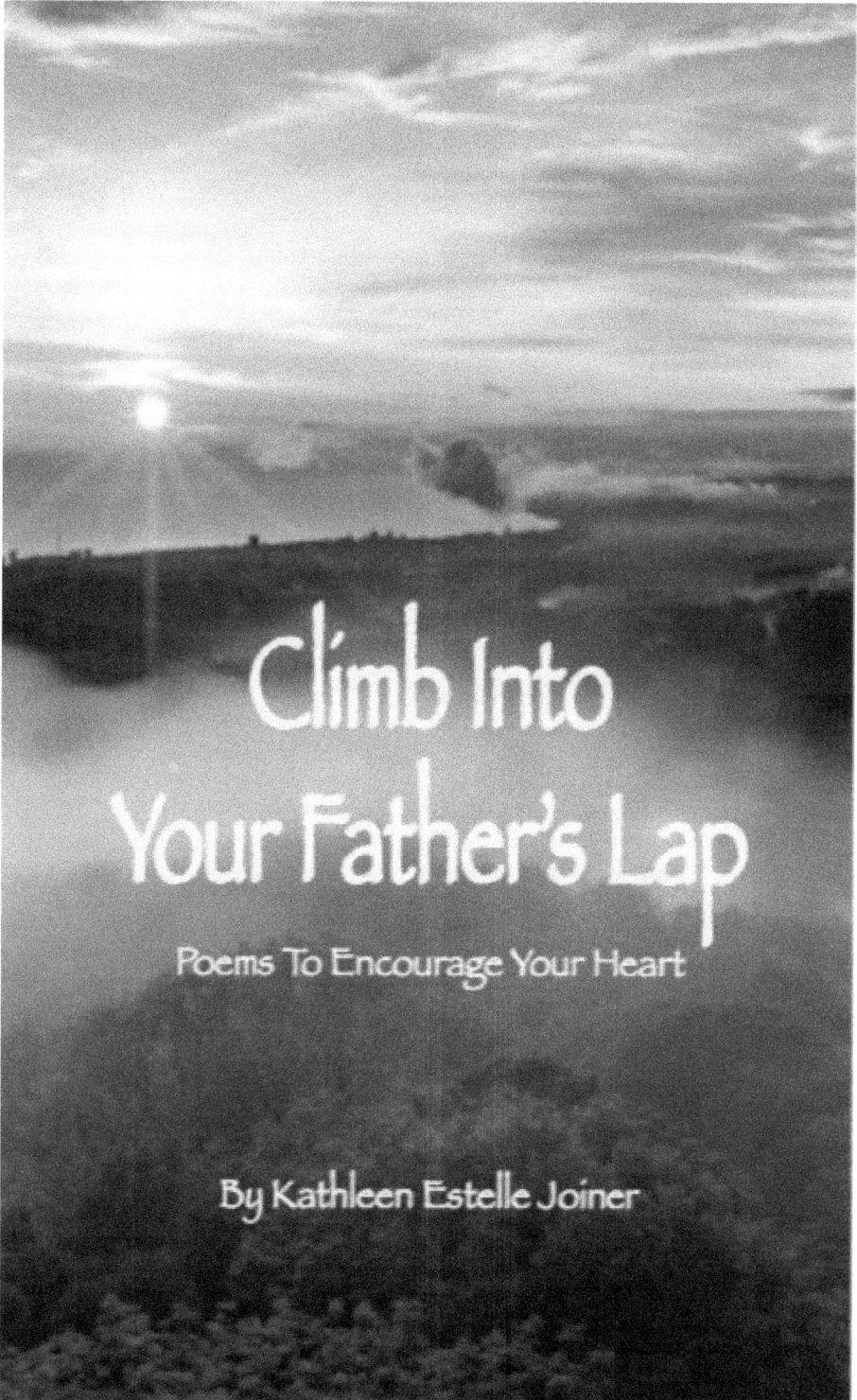

# Climb Into Your Father's Lap

## Poems To Encourage Your Heart

### By Kathleen Estelle Joiner

*The Treasured Box*

# Climb Into Your Father's Lap

## Poems To Encourage Your Heart

Kathleen Estelle Joiner

*The Treasured Box*

**Publisher**

"I AM" Publications
P.O. Box 355
West Union, Ohio 45693
E-mail preachers_dd4@yahoo.com

**Copyright**

**ISBN**

978-0-9857400-6-1

**Graphics**

Certain stock imagery © Thinkstock and are used for illustrative purposes only.

**Scripture**

Scripture taken from The Holy Bible, King James Version, Public Domain.

**Views**

Because of the dynamic nature of the Internet, any links contained in this book have changed and are no longer valid. The view expressed in this work are solely those of the author and do not necessarily reflect the reviews of the publisher, and the publisher hereby disclaims any responsibility for them.

# Dedication

This is dedicated to Mama and Daddy, my family, extended family and friends.

To all those who have poured into me; directly and indirectly.

To all those who have given me a reason or cause to climb into my Father's lap.

# Introduction

As we traverse on our journey, we will encounter "top of the mountain and below the valley lows" experiences.

During those tough times, we desperately search for a refuge to escape the tumultuous winds.

If we climb into our Father's lap we find a place of solace and peace. Where groans are understood and tears are welcomed and honored. A place where we can trust He will replenish our bankrupt faith and flat-lined spirit.

This is the secret place that Psalm 91:1-4 heralds:

"He that dwelleth in the secret place of the most High shall abide under the shadow of the almighty. I will say of the Lord, He is my refuge and my fortress: my God, in Him will I trust. Surely He shall deliver you from the snare of the fowler[a] And from the perilous pestilence. He shall cover you with His feathers, And under His wings you shall take refuge."

I thank my sister, Minister Roanna LaCour for encouraging me to seek His face.

According to 2nd Timothy 1:9 "We have been called according to His purpose (prosthesis or thesis, story). Who hath saved us, and called us with an holy calling, not according to our works, but according to his own purpose and grace, which was given us in Christ Jesus before the world began."

He has written our story before the foundation of the world. Our Creator had you and I in mind before the world began, and equipped us with grace to assure the victorious completion of our assignment. Thank you, Pastor Cecilia Jackson for your insightful teaching on the Heir Force.

As I spend time with our Father, I find He is intentional. He gives me instructions, strategies, promises. He is relational and shows me how to be a reconciliation link or conduit for healing. He helps me be an answered prayer. He gives me poetry; tunes my ears and re-focuses my sight for His will.

Some of these poems are popular, others debut in this book. All have given me hope and a release of despair; answered questions, exchanged mourning for a garment of praise. This was especially challenging as I said goodbye to many friends and family. In each tender season of grief, I climbed into His lap, emptied my soul and eventually found peace. I didn't necessarily find all the answers, but He showed compassion as I experienced His sovereignty.

In the surrendering, I found forgiveness and healing. I've found there is a balm in Gilead. I can grieve in hope. The Creator of the Universe cares when my heart is shattered and breathes hope into my deflated spirit. Daily. And when I can't muster the strength, He scoops me up and places me there.

He's taught me to trust His stillness. It's not quiet indifference ... rather it is silent intercession. It is then that He is working behind the scenes, on my behalf.

May this collection impart hope, rekindle your anticipation. While you are on your journey, be certain of this – absolutely nothing can separate you from God's love.

I invite you to climb into your Father's lap today. When you climb down, you will never be the same.

# Climb Into Your Father's Lap
Poems To Encourage Your Heart

## Table of Contents

*The Treasured Box*

# Climb Into Your Father's Lap

When you get hurt, climb into your Father's lap.
When you get bruised, climb into your Father's lap.
When you are worn and battle fatigued, climb into your
Father's lap.


He will scoop you up so close, to cradle you and rock you,
Comfort your hurts away.

He will wrap His loving arms around you and pour in the Oil.
As you cry and release your hurts, your tears mix with the Oil,
To soothe, to replace and heal.

It takes a while, so He allows you to sit on His fatherly lap as
long as you need it.
To soak up and replenish the supply of love you shed
As you were damaged.

When you are mended and refreshed
He kisses your tear-soaked face, hugs you,
And whispers, "I love you, my child," ever so gently.


As you climb down, He smooths your clothes,
Pats your head and smiles, as you whisper,
"Thank you, Abba Father."

When you get hurt, climb into your Father's lap.
When you climb down, you will never be the same.

Why don't you climb - right now,
into your Father's lap?

This poem was written in honor of my father, Clarence Wellborn Dabney, a flight engineer in the U.S. Air Force. He served with distinction in the Pacific during WWII, earning a Purple Heart.

When he returned home from a flight mission, Daddy found me hysterical after discovering my favorite Raggedy Ann doll was dismembered by a sibling.

I frantically gathered up the arms, legs and head and showed it to him, and sobbed, "Can't you fix it?"

This giant of a man, scooped me up in his arms, found Mama's sewing canister, and put me in his lap. As I snuggled under his chin, I was comforted by his steady heart beat and the scent of Aqua Velva after shave.

He wiped my tears, realigned the doll's stuffing and using various sizes of safety pins, reattached the limbs and the head.

Although the head was lopsided, my treasured possession was whole. My 5 year-old world was in order again.

If climbing on my natural father's lap can make such a difference, just imagine what happens when we bring our brokenness to our eternal Father.

He's waiting ...

# Do I Matter To The Universe?

How important am I to the universe?
In this world of people from sea to sea
We're important to the universe
Because He breathed life into you and me.

Yes, the world is crowded with people in excess of a billion
But it wouldn't matter if it was a gazillion and three
Because we are important to God
Yes, little ol' you and little ol' me.

We are important – collectively and individually, you see
We're important because we can change the world
Yes, little ol' and little ol' me.

He breathed life into our being
To transfer His power, His strength
His compassion and healing.

To better the world in time by one person or family
We have a divine purpose in this world –
Yes, little ol' you and little ol' me.

This world needs His wisdom and His vision
We are here to carry out His purpose and His mission.

Yes, the world is filled with people from sea to shining sea
But the world can't change itself;
It's crying out for laborers,
Yes, little ol' you and little ol' me.

In this universe, filled with people short and tall,
We are equipped to carry out a vision
You see, we're really not small at all.

For with us, He can change the universe.

# Children or Trees – I Created Them All

Children are just like the variety of trees.
Some of them have leaves,
Some have none
But they are fed and pruned by one Source
For I am the only One.

I nurture them to grow
Whether short or tall.
I know all their needs
And supply them all.

I know what makes them strong
I know which trees make shade
And those children - I know which ones rebel
And which ones behave.

Some of them appear fragile, and maybe sometimes weak
Others look strong with amazing physique.
Whether they're full of leaves
Or their trunks are almost bare,
I am their Source to provide their guidance and their care.

I know their potential, my breath into them I breathed
Their destiny is preserved within, in the tiny, little seed.
But know even when it's the winter season and no one
seems to be around
I am feeding them richly, but well beneath the solid ground.

So while you may not see Me, I am in plain view
I reside in those who revitalize their spirits
like the morning dew;
Others who have an assignment,
whose paths are destined to cross
You see I have designed it that no child shall be lost.

So whether snowy times or sunny blue skies ahead
I am the one who supplies. I am their daily bread.
I know each molecule, each cell and all the needs.
Remember I am their Source.
I am the air they breathe.

And in the wintery seasons,
Those uncertain times when you're unsure whether
they'll break or bend
I will send comfort, I will send them a friend.

And in that time, grace and mercy is released.
And during that time, I hear your prayers of deliverance,
and torment to cease.
I provide solace to the wounded, sick soul
And with bountiful grace, they are made whole.

And as this happens, they gain strength
and stronger, taller they stand
And they produce fruit and shade
throughout the whole land.

So from a frail twig, so tiny and so small
Appearing so weak, with no potential at all
God breathed life and gave a solid foundation
So now the tree provides shade and fruit
For all generations.

So remember whether a tree or a daughter or son
I created them all
And I love each one
Just like they were my single, only, one.

So rest easy father, sleep peacefully mother
For there have been no blunders.
Yes, you love them dearly
But I love them unconditionally, like no other.

# Did I Miss You?

In the busyness of my day
Did you say "turn left"
And I turned the wrong way?

In the intensity of my meetings
Did I miss the memo
That my life as I know it
Would be put on hold?

In the middle of a 'good word'
Was there some fine print
Or another instruction that wasn't heard?

In my quest to run after you
Did I get too ambitious and run past you?

No, my child, you haven't missed Me
You haven't run past the signs that direct you where to go
I've just switched the signs and changed
the speed limit to "slow."

That fast lane of traffic – once exactly the right speed
Has accelerated your gifts and planted your seeds
Now it's time for the harvest to show
And if you're going too fast, you'll miss it, you'll never know

The impact you've had on people you've met.
So yes, when I said "turn left",
I didn't mean 'your other left.'

You've been hearing correctly, my child, for Heaven's sake
I have not forsaken, I've just put on the brakes.

Keep trusting and declaring My name
No matter how it looks, you won't be ashamed.

No, my child, you have not missed me.
I am looking past your present and
Escorting you into your destiny.

# Follow The Star

Still today, we follow the Star
To seek His wisdom and find His heart.
It's all in the shiny, that wonderful star.

Wise men of old followed its gleam
To rescue them from an evil ruler – as told in a dream.
God's love and direction told them to look up and far
To pursue their deliverance through the bright, shining star.

For in darkness, does the star shine bright,
To dispel dissention, corruption and heart breaking strife.
Its gleam, its distinct focus of light
Bids us to look higher, to keep hope in sight.

For He promises never to leave nor forsake His own
Though at times we don't feel Him, we are never alone.
When we follow the star,
we cannot focus on our steps of the earth.
For each step draws us closer to our destiny's birth.

And stillness surrounds the star.
We find Him and we bow to the King
Though an infant, He is destined to be Lord of everything.
The star, brightly shimmering
Helps us find our way back to our King.

The babe, King of Kings, His cradle is love
Surrounded by everlasting faithfulness, straight from above.
Blanketed in peace and laid in a bed of straw.
Surroundings fitting for barn animals, not for a King at all.

The straw, remnants, rejected stalks of plants
Was hardly the beginnings for the Babe to advance
To the King, Lord of everything.

*The Treasured Box*

His beginnings are a sign
That He was born for the hopeful and the hopeless
For those who have it together, or entangled in a mess.
Those who are physically and mentally well,

Those who are shackled in a physical or mental hell.
Those who can afford anything at any cost
And those who are hopeless, forgotten and lost.

So, look up. Sharpen your focus. Search for the star
He will find and lead you ... from right where you are.
He will guide and direct you very, very far.
Search the sky, look in your heart, follow the star.

# I Like Me For Me

I have decided that I like me.
I like the way I smile
I like the way I go the extra mile.
I like me for me.

I like the way I protect.
I like the manner in which I expect
And even though some may scorn
Sometimes I like blowing my own horn.
I like me for me.

I like the way I minimize.
I like the way I maximize.
I like the way I fantasize.
I really like me for me.

I like the way I motivate.
I enjoy the way I cultivate.
And the dreams I dream,
Boy, are they great.
I really, really like me for me.

I like the way I show concern.
I am always amazed at what I discern.
I am usually open to receive, to learn.
I thank God for me.

I like the way that I can see
What is not – as though it will be.
I know what God has for me
Is really for me.
I am secure in me.

I like the way God's love shines through me
It glows so bright the world can see
That I love God, and He loves me.
And because of that, I love me for me.

## Just In Case

Just in case you are wondering if I love you.
Just in case you are wondering how I see
you from a Father's point of view.
In answer to your question -
I have always loved you.
And I still do.

Just in case you are asking if your sins can block
me from loving you again.
Or just in case you ask if I consider
You my daughter, my friend.
Just in case you are wondering - I cherish you.
My love will never end.

You are my beloved, my daughter,
the apple of my eye.
I see you when you are happy, and I see
you when you cry.
I've always loved you and am waiting for your reply
As I ask to enter your heart and eternally reside.

This chapter right here is not the story's end.
As you surrender to me, new chapters can begin.
I will lift you up and lovingly collect your
Heart pieces that are shattered
Just in case you are wondering why:
Because my beloved one, to Me, you matter.

You matter and your life's future does too.
Your plans are for a bright future,
Ideas to prosper and establish you.
And while I am yet working on your behalf,
invisible I may seem
But believe me, my child, I am interceding
and working behind the scenes.

*Just In Case ...*

Orchestrating events, and preparing hearts
of those you have not yet seen.
Guarding your heart and protecting you
from dangers seen and unseen.
Dispatching angels to minister to your
battle fatigued soul
Guiding you to restore your relationships,
to make you all the way whole.

While some may see disappointments and failures
of your past tests
When I gaze upon you daughter, I only see the best.
I see you taking steps on this journey, and upon
eagle's wings you can mount.
I see you making progress. Because believe me,
baby steps really do count.
I see you gaining strength, stamina and peace too.
I see you dreaming big, being laser focused
and blessings over taking you!

I see you kicking out doubt as they hang on for the ride.
For now you trust Me more, as I walk by your side.

So, just in case you are wondering if anything can
separate Me from you – heaven's no!
Absolutely nothing – nothing from on high,
and certainly nothing below.
Nothing created, nor demons. No past, present
and no powers from above.
Absolutely nothing can separate you from my love.

Finally, just in case you are wondering what happens
when I gaze upon your face.
I leap for joy, sing songs over you and grant you
heaps of grace to finish this race.

I love you today and always.
In case you are wondering. Just in case.

# No Matter The Circumstances, We Are Family

What is important to you
May not be important to me.
But when the day is over, we are still family.
Families have values and stick-to-it, too.
Families are made of me, and we are made of you.

We are all different, with wonderful gifts of various degrees,
And at the end of the day, we are still family.

We were nurtured under the same roof,
and yet have distinct personalities,
But we need one another to survive. For we are family.

We didn't choose each other, but God knew our needs
He molded us and knitted our hearts together.
He blessed our unit and called it family.

We have gone through many trials
and endured many a test too.
But you couldn't have triumphed
without me; and me without you.

We stand on each other's shoulders
and lift up each other to see
There is indeed hope for tomorrow,
for we are family.

For He knows where we are – whether local
or in the Alaskan deep blue seas.
There will be no one left behind.
We are glued tightly together. We are family.

There will be disagreements, some "fall out" fights too,
Some decisions require forgiveness, to restore relationships
anew.

## The Treasured Box

When the dust settles and we stand toe to toe.
We look at the big picture and somehow we still know.


That come hell or high water, we will survive the pressures of the stormy seas,
We are knitted together, our roots run very deep.
We are family.

# Sin Doesn't Live Here Anymore!

When I gave my life to Christ, I swept away my old habits,
Washed down the walls of my soul
And vacuumed the dust and debris of my life.

I then hung a sign out for the devil to see –
"Sin doesn't live here anymore."

It replaced the welcome mat that lay outside my door,
The place where the devil had frequented and had full reign.
When I turned my life over to Christ, I snatched up the mat
that said "Welcome" and replaced it with "Sin doesn't live
here anymore."

When the devil realized that he was evicted
without a 30 days' notice,
He was fighting mad. He peered through the windows
of my heart
And saw Love, which replaced hate.

He saw in the mirror of my eyes –
hope where there was despair.

He saw joy in the depths of my heart,
which had previously housed depression.
Inside my heart hung a sign,
"Sin doesn't live here anymore."

When the devil saw the new residents,
he knocked at the windows,
Rattled the door and even climbed the roof
to peek down the chimney.
He found every entrance sealed tight that was usually
Open for his comings and goings.

He pressed his nose to the window and rapped at the
window pane.

*The Treasured Box*

When he realized he had lost the war
and the Lord was the victor,
He kicked the dirt and had a fit.

And as he rolled around in the dirt and kicked his feet,
I shouted,
"You don't have any reign here,
because sin doesn't live here anymore!"

# Grant Me Patience, Lord

Give me patience, Lord. Let me know the way.
For I am tired and weary, and I've not the words to say.

Grant me patience, Lord. For it is only You who knows
My thoughts, my joys, my hurts, my inner need to grow.

My world right now is shaky, Lord. And many things
seem so unsure.
The things I place my faith in give me only pain to endure.

So I must ask you to be patient with me Lord,
Because You know I falter and fall. Many times I feel lost;
not alive at all.

Help me to keep a clean heart, one not consumed
with anger or hate.
Because it is very hard to refuse to be Satan's mate.

Help me to go on trusting and not to go into a shell.
You know when I'm hurt, I retreat. And being lonely
is pure hell.

But you know how much I can bear and again
You ask me to step out on faith.
You say in your hand, your guiding hand, I shouldn't
fear evil. I'll always be safe.

So teach me patience, Lord. Help me tolerate the
way of the land
Help me change whatever I can, and leave the rest
in Your almighty hands.

I love you Lord. And many times I don't thank you enough.
You are my bridge over troubled waters, my anchor
when things get rough.

So I'll keep on trusting and believing. I know you'll
teach me the way
To love, to share, to care for others, in my very
special way.

I'm going to close now, Lord.  And, please be assured
of my faith.
'Cause I need patience, Lord.
Oh, Lord, I can't wait.

So give me, no, grant me patience, Lord. So I might
walk your road
I walk it blindly. And carry such a heavy load.

I walk it softly. With a firm and solid conviction
That you are Lord, my only God always, without
worldly restrictions.

Grant me patience, Lord. And you know I want it right now.
But I know it is You, not I who controls the Plan Divine

So Lord, don't blink. Oh don't you dare.
You know I need that constant love and everlasting care.

## Say Yes – His Trust Is Your Anchor

God wants us to be obedient – even when it hurts.
As He leads us down a path that is for our best interest,
Many times it is uncomfortable, even painful
But, yet He asks for our obedience.

In submitting to Him, in giving our obedience,
He protects us, strengthens and builds us
Up for the greater Plan He has for us.

The darkness is but for a season.
His joy is everlasting.

As we go through the storms
We are rocked to and fro
Tossed around a bit, too.

But as long as we remain
Anchored in His Word,
We have the strength, faith and wisdom
To know God is the captain of the ship,
And He will not allow us to be ship wrecked.

And when the storm subsides,
The clouds dissipate and the Sun returns,
We have evidence that
God's love is all we need to live.

He is our rescuer, our Rock.
Our Anchor.
And yes, He is our Father.

## Hallie - A Prayer Warrior,
## A Valuable Friend

[Since Christmas, 2016, the Lord began preparing my heart for Hallie's transition. Not willing to accept it, He was so gracious to give me this poem in bite-size pieces, so I could digest it and have peace. About a week before she passed, He gave me the final words. Here is a tribute to a fierce prayer warrior, and a loving, faithful friend.]

There is an unwritten, but recorded true value of a friend.
One who is God-fearing, strong and faithful to the very end.

A friend who is insightful, constructive and prophetic too.
One who is fun and thoughtful... and reveals the God in you.

There's true value of a friend who has a third eye to see the future of things – right in full view.
And has the boldness to help you get your spiritual and natural breakthrough.

A friend who is quick to pray
and hold rock steady to His solid word.
And if you were slow in catching the good news, she'd say,
"What's wrong with you. Haven't you heard?"

A soldier who knows that her fingers are made for war
and will always say,
"Girl, the Lord is faithful. It may take us awhile, but it just don't take Him all day."

Hallie was a valuable friend, willing to talk to you, regardless of the occasion.
And ask you anytime if you are certain of your salvation.

Always searching for fun things for the Kingdom and not interested in slumber,
Continually expecting God's miracles, signs and wonders.

She was a fearless leader, unpretentious, smart, and ready to stand with you toe to toe.
And would say, "If you didn't know before, now you know."

And was she just another pretty face? Well, you know
that's just a myth.
She would get you straight and declare,
"Guess you didn't know who you are messing with."

For this is the day that the Lord has made. I WILL rejoice
and be glad ... For her friendship, leadership, her pouring
into us ... and all those sentiments.
But most of all, for her wisdom and Godly encouragement.

And now we surrender. We honor this time
we shared this earthly space.

We celebrate that our Lord in Heaven has said to Hallie,
"Welcome, faithful servant, into this place."
Congratulations, Hallie!

# My Love Is Custom Designed For You

My love is custom designed just for you
Because you are my child.

My love is designed especially for you
Because I know what you need.

Just like matching fingerprints,
My love is a perfect match for your desires.

Whatever the need, my love abounds
To fill the need and strengthen
my relationship with you.

Just as a mother knows her baby's cry,
I hear your cry and rush to quiet your fears,
Calm your anxiety.

Your concern is my concern.
Let me know your desires
And my everlasting love
Will fill the need and bind you
Closer to me.

For my love is specially made – just for you.

## It Still Ain't Over Soldiers -
## *Tribute To Our Champion, Linda Radford*

All through her life, Linda praised her Father with her gifts and obedience, an eternal difference she yearned to make.

And when she was aware of the illness, she took up the cross.  She did not hesitate.

So into the battle she went,
with partners of prayer at her side.
She strategically approached the enemy's camp and
showed Her Father's love – to those both far and wide.


Through her determination, she brought deliverance, though some times were disappointing, she brought His anointing, through times of despair, she showed God's love and compassion cannot compare.

Her different treatment centers were her mission field to show that this life is "temporal."
"Girl, you want to work for what's eternal,"
she'd attest.
So now she is dancing with her eternal Father –
it's what she loved best.
Telling Him of his goodness,
hearing the heartbeat of His chest.
Through the heartache and the suffering, she marched on, she pressed in, she travailed on.
She finished her course. She has passed her test.

No it still ain't over soldiers.
She shined her light, she ran her course.
She brought many alongside.
She completed it with her signature style and smile -
which was a mile wide.

She found that secret place of shelter,
protection where she could seek His face.
It was there she was refueled to give His strength,
power, mercy and grace.

She did it afraid. She did it in pain. She did it with joy.
She kept her eye on the prize.
She showed us how it was done.
So yes, dear saints, the battle is still won.

She is now praising her Father, dancing with her
Daddy, on streets of silver and gold.
Her life exemplified strategies of victory.
Regardless of the circumstances, God is still in control.

So now, we join her, lifting our
hands in praise,
surrendering our everything.
She is absent from the body,
but present with the Lord,
worshiping Her King.

Yes, we will miss this brightlight, this strong,
solid soldier of grace.
But it still ain't over.

Our Champion Linda Radford showed us how
to finish this race.
It Still Is Not Over!  We win!

# When We Ask For A Rebuilding

When we ask God for rebuilding of our character, or
ourselves,
God honors our request – with love.

First He loosens the first layers of consciousness,
Gently stripping away ourselves.
Much like when we peel an onion,
We cry because the peeling hurts and stings.

The second layer is a little more tender,
easier to tear away.

Finally God reaches the core –
Our roots, our spirit, our treasure chest
Of stored and hidden thoughts and emotions.

Gently, God pares away negative thoughts,
unhealthy habits,
Destructive deeds that stunt our growth and our
relationship with Him.

Then God gently rebuilds our character,
Slowly transforming us from within!

So when the rebuilding is complete,
A truly new creature of Christ abounds –
A true example of God's tremendous, victorious Love!

# How Desperate Are You?

How desperate are you?
How far will you run after me
How long will you look for me
Pursue me, chase after me and My Word?

How often will you move the debris
from your mind
To seek the light that shows your path
To give you the right direction on the
crossroads of your mind.

Do you have the endurance,
the stamina to climb the mountains
Of those that I won't move out of your way?
Will you ask for hinds feet of a deer -
To pull yourself up, to extend every ounce of
your energy
To get to the next mountainous crevice that takes you to
that Secret Place.

How high will you look up,
How low will you bow down to honor me?
Not for what I do, but for Who I am?

Are you desperate enough
To praise me through your pain
Through the endless heartache
Through the shattered, broken pieces
Of a dream – delayed- not denied?

Are you desperate enough?
To be satisfied with a piece of understanding and peace
To hold onto the pieces of My plan that I share -
in My time.

My plans are to prosper you,
to give you a good future
But I cannot share everything at once.
Each piece, each morsel is an important step
In the process of healing, hoping,
Restoring faith, increasing your trust in Me.

For I am the Lord, thy God. You shall not have other gods
before Me.

When you are desperate, you are not busy
running around.
You are seeking, waiting, expecting.
That is when the slightest move from Me,
The smallest voice, the tiniest whisper grabs your attention.
Your desperation heightens your senses.
Your desperation fine tunes your hearing ear
for My Word.

For you know – one word from Me changes the situation.
One word from Me changes night into day.
One Word turns the key
To set the captives free!
Just one Word!

You know, daughter that just a breath from Me
Breathes life, refreshing into a deep, frozen dream.
A dream so far buried in the recesses of your mind
That it no longer registers a thought, a consideration
or acknowledgement
So far buried it requires the Holy Spirit
with the radar, laser to pinpoint it and
Call it forth like Lazarus from the grave.

Are you desperate enough for the
End result of freedom, true peace and joy -
That goes beyond your understanding?

So desperate that you go through the painful peeling of
Secret thoughts, sabotaging habits,
buried and festering hurts?

The pain is not in vain.
It is your investment in your liberation.
It is your milestone in the journey
to freedom.
It is the scaling of the mountain of joy and peace.

At the top of the mountain
You'll discover the tears were fuel for your determination
Your praise was your bearing down,
the pushes to your breakthrough
Your worship was your war cry to your wonderful,
supernatural acceleration
To the throne room of treasures from the heart
of your Lord, your King.

So remain consistently desperate.
Keep your ear tuned to my voice.
Keep your tongue bridled.
Keep your eyes focused, your praise laser pointed
towards Me.
Stand still. Watch me fight for you.
Endure, be determined in seeking Me;
not in doing deeds, or repairing people.
For I am the ultimate Fixer.
Once I'm in the midst of a situation, it is not just fixed,
it is eternally restored.

Pace yourself, for it is a process.
But a process of tearing down, peeling away,
pruning and restoration in Me.

The Prince of Peace, Wonderful Counselor,
the almighty, Everlasting Father.
For I exchange beauty for ashes.
The heaviness of spirit for the garment of praise.


Be desperate in Me.  Be continually desperate for Me.

## Keep Pressing On

Don't you know I love you?
Don't you know I'm always with you –
Especially when you don't feel it?

Let the tears flow – they will heal you.
Carry your broken heart to me
I'll pour in the oil and wine,
Mend the cracks and breathe
New life into the crevices of your being.

Trust me. My love will help your wounds.
Daily apply the salve of forgiveness to the wound.
Cast your caress on me. Press on. Press into me.
Believe in miracles – for I believe in you.

I pray for you. I have your best interest at heart.
You are my child.

Let me rock you to sleep, comfort you.
Help you soothe the hurts.
This pain, loneliness and uncertainty
is for a short season.

If you stand and remain anchored in Me,
You won't break as the enemy desires.
You'll succeed in spite of the trials because
I am with you.

When you stand firm, I keep you in the hollow
of My hand
To give you peace and joy – unspeakable joy!

Stand in the midst of the storm.
Raise your hands and praise Me!
Exercise your faith – this keeps you strong

In your expectations of My blessings and miracles.

Your storm is almost over and you are still standing –
Because you are my child!

My children far more than a conqueror.
They are amazingly victorious!

## Thanks For Knotting My Rope Of Faith

Thanks for knotting my rope of faith
And allowing me to hang on.

Thanks for knotting my rope of faith
And letting me shimmy my way to safety.

Thanks for knotting my rope of faith
And letting me be an example
That faith is evidence of things unseen
And that God's Word is always true.

Thanks for knowing when I could not find
The strength to knot the rope.
Thanks for extending your hand and knotting it for me.

Thanks for letting me hang onto your strength
Until I could muster enough to go through
Another hour, another month, another season.

Jesus is Lord. Jesus is still on the throne.
Yes, prayers still changes situations!

Lord, thanks for being my rope holder!

# Lord, I Thank You

Lord, thanks for affirming me
When others are denouncing me.

Thank you for uplifting me
When others are abusing me.

Thank you for loving me
When others are destroying me.

Lord, thank you for loving me
When others are despising me.

Thanks for declaring I am an heir of the Kingdom
Even when I feel like an orphan.

Thank you for urging me to believe, to expect miracles
Even when the day is blacker than black.

Thanks for granting me stability in knowing that joy
Will indeed come in the morning
And that strength and hope will rise with the morning
sun.

Thanks for arming me with the power of prayer
Even when I can barely whisper "Jesus."

Thanks for giving me the strength to tear down
strongholds,
Even when I can barely lift my hands to praise your
Name.

Lord, you are my light in the middle of darkness.
You are my anchor in the midst of the storm.

Your love abounds so angels can be dispatched
When my enemies stalk me and are encamped around
me.

Thank you for being the Alpha and Omega,
For the breath of life and strumming a song for my
heart to sing.
Thank you Lord, for being my everything.

# Thank You For Grandparents

Thank you for grandparents who tug your pony tails,
Wiggle your nose and tell you bedtime stories.

Thank you for grandparents who smooth your dress
after a fall,
Smile at you to make you grow from tiny to tall.

Thank you for grandparents who are truly grand in
their love,
Supreme in dishing out esteem,
Outstanding in scooping on that extra helping of love
only a grandparent can hold.

Thank you for grandparents who instill those values
that endure generation after generation
For seeing me as an important part of your future
An essential part of your universe.

Thank you for grandparents, who enjoy you for you,
Not for the expectations that can sometimes muddle
the mirror of self.

Thank you for grandparents who hold you while you
are babies
Then hold you dear in their hearts as you grow older.

Thank you for grandparents who never age, their love
is as new as the day
You made your grand entrance into the world.

Lord, thank you for grandparents – who love.

## CDs For Hugs*
### (Tribute To Pastor Brown's Mom)

A mother's love never ceases.
Always discerning the signs while hearing
the Master's voice.
Leaving directions for the family, standing firm
in her choice.
She would confidently take her cares
to the Lord in prayer.
Her wisdom of the Word and love of God, she was
always willing to share.

A mother, an aunt, a grandmother,
and a great grand too,
She exuded grace, wisdom and a pleasant point of view.
She held many titles, but she was the only one
Whose smile could be payment for a CD of her favorite
pastor, her son.

At the end of service, we'd wait for her to make her way
to the Tape Room Door.
She'd say, "You've made CDs of my favorite pastor. Do
you have any more?
"Of course, we do. "We're saving one,
especially just for you."
"Oh thank you", she'd smile
as her eyes twinkled brightly.
Then she'd ask, "What do I owe you?" oh, so politely.

The answer remained the same. "Nothing but a hug."
"Oh, I can manage that. Yes sir, in Jesus' name."
And we'd collect her hug in exchange for her gift.
But we received an extra boost of faith.
Her hugs gave our spirits such a lift.

So, for now, we'll give hugs in her precious memory.
Pastor Brown - God handpicked your mom,
On purpose – for your legacy and to fulfill your destiny.

  * Joint Copyright with Mary George - Used By Permission

## You Are Invited To The Ultimate Happy, Refreshing Hour

Following a day packed with emotional and
spiritual distress
I visited the Intercessory Prayer Service
And immediately found a refreshing, an anointed rest.

All the mind blowing worries melted away
In His Presence, they just could not stay.

His love gushed through my spirit and calmed
my anxieties
My negative feelings and emotions broke away.
And His Peace, joy and sweet contentment remained.

What peace! What joy, what anointing reside
His Holy, manifested Presence clearly abides.

A holy refreshing waits just for you,
When you visit the powerful Prayer Service,
You're sure to experience it too!

[Prayer written at the old Prentice Building]

## Sitting At Your Feet

Being seated at your feet
Is the best place to be
To soak up your wisdom and powerful energy
Siting at your feet gives me the ultimate victory.

For at your feet
Is the ultimate place for me – to place all my worries,
hurts and petitions
And leave them there
For your divine instruction and intervention.

For at your feet
I surrender my will, I sacrifice my defeats
It is at this special, humbling place
That I receive my victory.

At your feet
You give me strength and courage to stand
At your feet, I find an anchor,
I find forgiveness and salvation;
For which I am glad.

At your feet, your precious feet
I find joy, comfort and soul-soothing peace.

Lord, keep me at your feet.

## When You Wake Me To Say Good Morning

I ask You to spend more time with me
I asked You to do it soon.
But when I asked You to do it – I was thinking of
some time, like noon?

First I was sleeping soundly and suddenly I was not.
I pondered if You wanted to spend time with me.
Because I was sleepy, I said, "I hope not."

"It's too early to talk. Can't we do it another time?"
Like when I'm more awake,
and when the sun is shining?"

As I gathered my covers and attempted to regain my
favorite position,
I guiltily gathered my thoughts and needs
And began reciting them in a rehearsed petition.

I tossed and turned to re-enter my dream, while
getting slightly agitated.
As you stood there watching, and thinking, "Maybe I
should have waited."
Perhaps I should have waited until the sun was bright
And the sky a pretty hue.
Maybe I should have, but I wanted to share the
sunrise with you.

I longed to share a piece of my heart.
And lend you my ear, too.
I wanted to hug you and love you. And say that you
are special, too.

*The Treasured Box*

In the morning when the dew is new, yet before the
birds start to sing
I wanted to tell you "Good Morning"
and grant you everything.
So all of your problems and hurts –
from the biggest to the least
Could be placed on my shoulders –
in exchange for my heavenly peace.

I was so excited to get invited
Into your busy day. I wanted to get to you first
Before your time was scheduled away.

But today is not good for you, I can tell.
You push and brush me away.
I think our time together is precious.
You take it for granted, I'd say.

You feel because I am your Father
To fulfill your requests is an obligation.
But I cherish our time together.
To me it is a celebration.

It is when you can bring your heart to me –
when many times you are sad.
And during those times, your giants are slain;
without a rock or a rag.

It is time I equip you for the day.
When I send favor and peace abounding your way.

For it is not your words I seek,
but it is your heart I long.
The early fellowship is a treasure,
not punishment for deeds you've done wrong.

It is when the Lord gently kisses the Sun, and it
blushes a pretty pink, yellow and blue.
It is that special time He custom designs  -
especially just for you.

Whispered words of encouragement.
New mercies and discernment too.
Are all waiting in the early morning time –
spent with the Lord and you.
When He wakes you to say 'Good Morning.'

[Calling all the Champions – shared with Sis. Lucy Katenkamp, and Bro. Derrick Busch]

## A Tribute To Our Champions – Full Of Resolve And Resolution

This is for the Champions who look past the dismay, and prophesy to the situation with expectation, preparation and declare,

"This too shall pass. This pain and suffering just won't last. I will continually look to the hills from whence cometh my help. I will draw strength from my God. For I am not by myself."

For He says, His plans are for me for a good, bright future and tomorrow. And His gifts are rich and addeth no sorrow. And although in pain, I look to Him for my strength and courage to grow. For with His grace I can withstand life's sufferings and blows.

And though there are times when I feel I've been counted out, I know my feelings are not what my victory is about.

I remain confident in God's Promises, and not just religion. I dig within myself and Him. And I make a decision. A decision to gather my shattered dreams from the floor, and place them in the hands of my Father, whom I adore.

And this Creator, who created light by saying, "let there be," will keep me in His hands and declare unto me – "You are more than a conqueror; in Me you have the victory."

He has breathed new life into me and I will prophesy
to these dry bones, for I know He abides in me.
I am never alone. And those prophesies
command health, hope and restoration. And
remove impossibility from any difficult situation.

For He gathers His Promises and
mixes them with my faith,

And He gives me peace and strength to win
this race. As I release my fears and take His
Hand, I recall His thoughts for me out number
the grains of sand.

So, though at times, weak, my spirit takes a stand.
I WILL live for the next moment, the next hour.
He is the breath in my being. In me He
imparts His power.

So I keep my eyes and faith fixed on this as
I progress. He gives me peace, He gives me
sweet rest. And in this test, I refuse defeat. I
stand on His Promises – every one He
will undoubtedly keep.

His promise is for divine health and my body
whole. I look past the situation and declare,
"All is well with my soul!"

I will not give up – for I am a Champion!

## Afterword

Before the beginning of time, God had us each in mind. He had our journey already thought about and carved through the pages of time. Each chapter was written, every mountain climbed, every road charted. Every entrance ramp to put us back on track was already carved out. So before the world was created, God had great-grandmother Estelle, her family and their destiny charted and mapped.

And so it is with us. When we were born, angels were assigned to keep, protect, assist and escort us through all times, to our appointed end.

When Great grandmother Estelle was born, her talents and gifts were embedded in her DNA. She used the power of the pen to overcome numerous challenges, to encourage her in child bearing years, and turbulent economic times. The pen was her tool to encourage herself, family, and countless others who read her gems in her weekly column in the Oakland Tribune. This gift is benchmarked in her legacy.

So, after her death, the poetry was boxed and stored. Decades later it was presented to my mother, by her step mother, in California.

That box, hosted, carried, housed, and was a cardboard guardian to these poetic treasures. I believe from 1889 to 2019, great-grandmother's angels got with Mama's angels to help escort this box to my generation. Although Great grandmother Estelle had passed, her assignment of sharing her poetry was not complete. Until now.

Fifteen years ago, Mama gave it to me saying, "My grandma never got a chance to publish; maybe you can do something with them."

In that moment, the legacy was transferred. Although this was a physical impartation, all of the family members enjoy similar DNA gifts from Mama and Daddy, our ancestors.

Daddy was in the Navy and Air Force, an artist, and engineer. Mama and Daddy were both pillars for family, staunch advocates of education, caring for the youth and elderly. Philip was a Lieutenant Commander (USN), and an excellent teacher in VA. Remains a lover of science. Michael, has held local and international writing positions, enjoys a successful career in media/communications in CA.

Roanna's passion is teaching children and caring for senior citizens – with excellence and is an extremely awesome baker. Margaret, who is deceased, was compassionate and outstanding in youth social service. Kathleen excels in communications, publishing, teaching the power of the pen. Paul, NMD, Ph.D, is a naturopathic doctor in GA, offering holistic care; a passion stemming from Mom's love for plants and their healing components. Christopher cares for customers; teaches and trains team members. Steven teaches, supervises and leads in the governmental sector. This is our DNA.

This legacy is rooted in our children, cousins and family tree.

Each one of us has inherited a box; not necessarily a physical container, but God-designed passions and tools to enrich, empower and impact our families and future generations.

This collection of poetry speaks of the radiation of the Lord's love for us as it flows from Him, to His Son, Jesus Christ and the Holy Spirit. This love spills over into the hearts and minds of God's children.

It is my hope that these poetic words touch the heart of God as you bring your cares to Him and climb into your Father's Lap!

*Roanna LaCour*

### *Kathleen Estelle Joiner*

A Literary Locksmith, Kathleen reveals the power of the pen to unlock the stories within; to release, empower, declare the power of God's love in our lives.

"Everyone has a story, but no one can tell yours like you," Kathleen believes.

She began her writing career at the Journal Herald Newspaper. Her articles have been featured in local newspapers, and international magazines, Art & Living. Kathleen studied Communications at Wright State University and University of Cincinnati and her innate passion for communications is demonstrated in her professional life through print, online news writing, manuscript writing/editing, broadcasting in corporate and non-profit sectors.

She is the author of *Whispers of the Heart Healing Journal,* instructor of journaling, speaker at women's retreats and workshops.

She was born into a lineage of authors, including her (paternal) Great-grandmother, Estelle Beasley Turner, a weekly columnist for Oakland Gazette; and cousin, Wendell Philip Dabney, publisher and editor-in-chief of The Union, Cincinnati's oldest Black newspaper. The passion for writing is alive and well in their family tree.

Her favorite scripture is Romans 8:28, "We know all things work together for good to them that love God."

kathleenjoiner@yahoo.com
Website: https://wordsforyourgood.wordpress.com/

www.ingramcontent.com/pod-product-compliance
Lightning Source LLC
Chambersburg PA
CBHW071744090426
42738CB00011B/2556